THE LIBERATED WOMAN'S VOICE

365 Affirmations for the Mind, Body, & Soul

Bestselling Author
Maryann Rivera-Dannert

Copyright © 2025 Maryann Rivera-Dannert and MRD Empowerment Solutions, LLC
All rights reserved.

No part of this publication may be reproduced, stored in a retrieval system, or transmitted in any form or by any means, electronic, mechanical, photocopying, recording, or otherwise, without the prior written permission of the publisher, except by a reviewer who may quote brief passages in a review.

First Edition
ISBN: 979-8-9924069-1-7
Published by MRD Empowerment Solutions, LLC

Printed in the United States of America
For permissions, inquiries, or speaking engagements, contact: maryann@maryannriveradannert.com

This book is a work of nonfiction. The strategies, tools, and insights are based on the author's professional expertise and experience. While every effort has been made to ensure the accuracy and effectiveness of the content, the author and publisher make no guarantees and disclaim any liability for how the information is used or interpreted by readers.

Welcome, Beautiful Soul

If you are holding this book in your hands, it is not by accident. You were led here because a part of you is ready to heal, ready to rise, ready to fully step into the woman you were always meant to be. *Liberated!*

This book is for the woman who has carried more than her share. The woman who has poured into everyone else, while quietly forgetting herself. The woman who has fought battles no one saw or knew about, and who still shows up every day, even when she feels empty inside. The woman who longs for peace in her mind, freedom in her body, and light in her soul.

If that resonates with you, this book was written for you.

Inside these pages are 365 affirmations, one for every day of the year. Each is a reminder that you are worthy, loved, and more powerful than you realize. These affirmations are not just words on a page; they are daily seeds of truth, waiting to be planted in your heart and nurtured through your commitment to yourself.

When you choose to read an affirmation each day, and more importantly, when you decide to speak it, feel it, and embody it, you will begin to notice a shift.

- Your mind will begin to release old stories of doubt, fear, and comparison.

- Your body will respond to the love and respect you give it, moving with renewed energy and confidence.
- Your soul will awaken, guiding you into deeper alignment with who you truly are.

There is also a daily coaching question that aligns with the affirmation. This is for deeper work, because you were not created to be stuck and unfulfilled. You were designed to be fearless, free, happy, and *liberated*.

At the end, there are five reflection questions for you to consider. Answering each of them honestly, make sure to keep showing up for yourself and the higher version of you waiting on the other side.

This book is not about perfection. It's about presence. It's about showing up for yourself, one day at a time, and giving yourself the love, grace, and empowerment you so freely give to others.

By the end of these 365 days, you will not be the same woman who started. You will be more **rooted** in truth, more **empowered** in your choices, more **awakened** in your spirit, and more **liberated** in your life.

So take a deep breath, open your heart, and begin this journey. The transformation you desire begins the moment you decide you are worth showing up for and doing the work.

With love and anticipation for your journey,
Maryann

Day 1

My thoughts are powerful, and I choose ones that uplift me.

What's a thought you can repeat to yourself today to shift your energy?

_____

_____

_____

_____

_____

_____

_____

_____

_____

_____

Day 2

I release comparison and celebrate my unique path.

How can you honor yourself without measuring it against others?

_____

_____

_____

_____

_____

_____

_____

_____

_____

Day 3

I am capable of learning, growing, and evolving every day.

What's something new you can do today that will help you grow, even just a little?

_____

_____

_____

_____

_____

_____

_____

_____

_____

_____

Day 4

My mind is a safe place for peace and possibility.

What would peace look like in your thoughts right now?

_____

_____

_____

_____

_____

_____

_____

_____

_____

_____

Day 5

I let go of the past and make room for new beginnings.

What's one thing from your past you're finally ready to release with love?

_____

_____

_____

_____

_____

_____

_____

_____

_____

_____

Day 6

Clarity comes to me with ease when I slow down and listen.

Where can you pause today to allow clarity to naturally rise up?

_____

_____

_____

_____

_____

_____

_____

_____

_____

_____

Day 7

I am not my mistakes; I am my lessons and growth.

What lesson from your past are you now using as wisdom?

_____

_____

_____

_____

_____

_____

_____

_____

_____

_____

Day 8

My voice matters, and I speak my truth with confidence.

What truth have you been silencing that's ready to be spoken?

_____

_____

_____

_____

_____

_____

_____

_____

_____

_____

Day 9

I am led by faith, not fear.

What step could you take today if faith was your only guide?

_____

_____

_____

_____

_____

_____

_____

_____

_____

_____

_____

Day 10

I trust my intuition to lead me to aligned choices.

What decision do you already know the answer to deep down?

_____

_____

_____

_____

_____

_____

_____

_____

_____

_____

Day 11

Each challenge is an invitation for me to rise higher.

How can you use your current challenge to show yourself what you're made of?

_____

_____

_____

_____

_____

_____

_____

_____

_____

_____

Day 12

I am enough exactly as I am, right now.

What would you stop chasing if you fully
believed you were already enough?

_____

_____

_____

_____

_____

_____

_____

_____

_____

_____

Day 13

I choose courage over comfort, always.

What bold action can you take today, even if it feels uncomfortable?

_____

_____

_____

_____

_____

_____

_____

_____

_____

_____

Day 14

My creativity flows freely and without judgment.

What could you create today if you didn't worry about how it looked or sounded?

_____

_____

_____

_____

_____

_____

_____

_____

_____

_____

Day 15

I forgive myself for past choices and honor the wisdom they brought.

What's one thing you can thank your past self for teaching you?

_____

_____

_____

_____

_____

_____

_____

_____

_____

_____

Day 16

I focus on progress, not perfection.

What's one small win you can celebrate right now?

_____

_____

_____

_____

_____

_____

_____

_____

_____

_____

_____

Day 17

I am free from self-doubt and filled with self-belief.

What proof do you already have that you're capable and strong?

_____

_____

_____

_____

_____

_____

_____

_____

_____

_____

Day 18

Every day, I rewire my mind to align with my dreams.

What thought today reflects the woman living your dream life?

_____

_____

_____

_____

_____

_____

_____

_____

_____

_____

Day 19

My inner dialogue is gentle, loving, and affirming.

What would your self-talk sound like if you spoke to yourself like your best friend?

_____

_____

_____

_____

_____

_____

_____

_____

_____

_____

_____

Day 20

I am unstoppable when I align my thoughts with my purpose.

What thought right now helps you reconnect to your bigger "why"?

_____

_____

_____

_____

_____

_____

_____

_____

_____

_____

Day 21

I choose to see obstacles as opportunities.

What hidden opportunity might be sitting inside your current struggle?

_____

_____

_____

_____

_____

_____

_____

_____

_____

Day 22

I am worthy of peace and mental clarity.

What do you need to let go of to protect your peace today?

_____

_____

_____

_____

_____

_____

_____

_____

_____

_____

Day 23

My dreams are valid, and I take steps toward them daily.

What simple step can you take today that honors your dreams?

_____

_____

_____

_____

_____

_____

_____

_____

_____

_____

Day 24

I no longer shrink to fit; I expand to be seen.

Where in your life are you ready to show up fully and unapologetically?

_____

_____

_____

_____

_____

_____

_____

_____

_____

_____

Day 25

My resilience is stronger than any fear.

What's one moment that proves you've bounced back before, and can again?

_____

_____

_____

_____

_____

_____

_____

_____

_____

_____

_____

Day 26

I focus on what I can control and release the rest.

What can you lovingly hand over to faith instead of worrying about?

_____

_____

_____

_____

_____

_____

_____

_____

_____

_____

Day 27

I am constantly evolving into the best version of me.

What part of you is growing stronger or wiser right now?

_____

_____

_____

_____

_____

_____

_____

_____

_____

_____

Day 28

My thoughts create my reality, and I choose wisely.

What new thought would instantly shift how you see your day?

_____

_____

_____

_____

_____

_____

_____

_____

_____

_____

Day 29

I am a magnet for solutions, not problems.

What question could you ask that opens you to new answers?

_____

_____

_____

_____

_____

_____

_____

_____

_____

_____

Day 30

My future is brighter than my past.

What exciting possibility are you walking toward right now?

_____

_____

_____

_____

_____

_____

_____

_____

_____

Day 31

I am at peace with who I am becoming.

How can you show yourself grace while you're still in progress?

_____

_____

_____

_____

_____

_____

_____

_____

_____

_____

_____

Day 32

Confidence radiates from my thoughts into my actions.

What confident action can you take to match your mindset?

_____

_____

_____

_____

_____

_____

_____

_____

_____

_____

Day 33

I can rewrite my story at any time.

What part of your story are you ready to
rewrite with power and pride?

_____

_____

_____

_____

_____

_____

_____

_____

_____

_____

Day 34

I attract clarity, creativity, and calmness.

What would be your ideal environment to inspire creativity?

_____

_____

_____

_____

_____

_____

_____

_____

_____

_____

Day 35

I choose to focus on abundance, not lack.

What in your life reminds you that you already have more than enough?

_____

_____

_____

_____

_____

_____

_____

_____

_____

_____

_____

Day 36

I am grateful for my brilliant and capable mind.

What's one thing you've recently overcome?

_____

_____

_____

_____

_____

_____

_____

_____

_____

Day 37

I create space for new ideas to blossom.

What mental clutter can you release to make space for inspiration?

_____

_____

_____

_____

_____

_____

_____

_____

_____

_____

Day 38

I can do hard things and still thrive.

What challenge have you faced that showed your true strength?

_____

_____

_____

_____

_____

_____

_____

_____

_____

Day 39

My focus is sharp, and my vision is clear.

What distraction can you set aside to stay focused on what truly matters?

_____

_____

_____

_____

_____

_____

_____

_____

_____

_____

Day 40

I am not my fear; I am my faith in action.

What bold move would faith make on your behalf today?

Day 41

My mind is fertile ground for positive thoughts.

What empowering belief are you ready to plant and nurture?

_____

_____

_____

_____

_____

_____

_____

_____

_____

_____

Day 42

I am free to release beliefs that no longer serve me.

What outdated beliefs are you ready to change?

_____

_____

_____

_____

_____

_____

_____

_____

_____

_____

Day 43

My wisdom grows daily.

What recent experience has taught you something valuable about yourself?

_____

_____

_____

_____

_____

_____

_____

_____

_____

_____

Day 44

I let go of the need to control everything.

Where can you surrender and trust what's unfolding?

Day 45

I focus on the present moment with calm awareness.

What can you notice right now that brings you back to peace?

_____

_____

_____

_____

_____

_____

_____

_____

_____

_____

Day 46

My thoughts are aligned with love and possibility.

How can you choose love over fear in this moment?

_____

_____

_____

_____

_____

_____

_____

_____

_____

_____

Day 47

I create powerful outcomes with powerful thinking.

What do you think right now supports the outcome you want?

_____

_____

_____

_____

_____

_____

_____

_____

_____

_____

_____

Day 48

I am open to new ways of moving forward.

What's one situation you could view through a softer, wiser lens?

_____

_____

_____

_____

_____

_____

_____

_____

_____

_____

Day 49

I can trust my mind to guide me in the right direction.

When has your intuition been right before, and how can you trust it again?

_____

_____

_____

_____

_____

_____

_____

_____

_____

Day 50

My potential is limitless.

What dream have you been downplaying that deserves your attention?

_____

_____

_____

_____

_____

_____

_____

_____

_____

_____

Day 51

I no longer overthink; I act with clarity.

What decision can you make today instead of analyzing it again and again?

_____

_____

_____

_____

_____

_____

_____

_____

_____

_____

_____

Day 52

Every thought I choose brings me closer to freedom.

What freeing thought can you hold onto right now?

_____

_____

_____

_____

_____

_____

_____

_____

_____

_____

Day 53

I embrace curiosity and learning.

What are you curious about that you can lean into this week?

_____

_____

_____

_____

_____

_____

_____

_____

_____

_____

Day 54

I replace fear with faith in every decision.

What would your next choice look like if it was made from faith, not fear?

_____

_____

_____

_____

_____

_____

_____

_____

_____

_____

Day 55

My self-talk builds me up, never tears me down.

What loving words does your heart need to hear from you today?

_____

_____

_____

_____

_____

_____

_____

_____

_____

_____

Day 56

I find peace in letting go of overthinking.

What's one thing you can mentally release to feel lighter today?

_____

_____

_____

_____

_____

_____

_____

_____

_____

_____

Day 57

I am in charge of what I focus on.

What deserves your focus, and what doesn't?

_____

_____

_____

_____

_____

_____

_____

_____

_____

_____

Day 58

My thoughts fuel my confidence.

What thought instantly reminds you of your strength?

_____

_____

_____

_____

_____

_____

_____

_____

_____

_____

Day 59

I practice gratitude with every thought.

What's one thing, big or small, you're thankful for right now?

_____

_____

_____

_____

_____

_____

_____

_____

_____

_____

Day 60

My perspective is powerful and unique.

How can your unique way of seeing things serve or inspire others?

_____

_____

_____

_____

_____

_____

_____

_____

_____

_____

Day 61

I release the urge to compare myself.

What can you celebrate about your own progress today?

_____

_____

_____

_____

_____

_____

_____

_____

_____

_____

Day 62

I focus on the lessons, not the losses.

What lesson are you walking away with that made the struggle worth it?

_____

_____

_____

_____

_____

_____

_____

_____

_____

_____

Day 63

My mental clarity grows every day.

What daily habit helps clear your mind and center your thoughts?

_____

_____

_____

_____

_____

_____

_____

_____

_____

_____

Day 64

I trust my ability to find the answers.

How can you remind yourself that you've always figured things out before?

Day 65

My thoughts align with my highest vision.

What thought today connects you to your Higher Self?

_____

_____

_____

_____

_____

_____

_____

_____

_____

_____

Day 66

I create calm within chaos.

What practice helps you stay grounded when life feels messy?

_____

_____

_____

_____

_____

_____

_____

_____

_____

Day 67

I choose understanding over judgment.

Who or what needs your compassion instead of criticism?

_____

_____

_____

_____

_____

_____

_____

_____

_____

_____

_____

Day 68

My mind is sharp and full of possibility.

What new idea are you excited to explore next?

_____

_____

_____

_____

_____

_____

_____

_____

_____

Day 69

I let go of worry and invite trust.

What outcome can you release so you can rest in trust instead?

_____

_____

_____

_____

_____

_____

_____

_____

_____

_____

Day 70

My perspective shifts easily toward hope.

What's one hopeful thought you can hold when things feel uncertain?

_____

_____

_____

_____

_____

_____

_____

_____

_____

_____

Day 71

I am brave enough to think differently.

What bold idea are you ready to believe in, even if others don't?

_____

_____

_____

_____

_____

_____

_____

_____

_____

_____

Day 72

I allow my imagination to expand freely.

What would your dream life look like if you allowed yourself to imagine it fully?

_____

_____

_____

_____

_____

_____

_____

_____

_____

_____

Day 73

My thoughts inspire aligned action.

What inspired thought can you act on right now?

_____

_____

_____

_____

_____

_____

_____

_____

_____

_____

Day 74

I trust my mind to lead me with wisdom.

What is your inner wisdom gently nudging you toward today?

_____

_____

_____

_____

_____

_____

_____

_____

_____

_____

Day 75

I welcome fresh ideas into my awareness.

How can you make space for creativity to flow today?

_____

_____

_____

_____

_____

_____

_____

_____

_____

_____

Day 76

My intelligence is a gift I honor.

How can you use your knowledge to make something easier for yourself?

_____

_____

_____

_____

_____

_____

_____

_____

_____

_____

Day 77

I am free to see things in new ways.

What story about yourself are you ready to see with more grace and truth?

_____

_____

_____

_____

_____

_____

_____

_____

_____

_____

_____

Day 78

I practice mental stillness with ease.

How can you create a quiet moment just for your mind today?

_____

_____

_____

_____

_____

_____

_____

_____

_____

_____

Day 79

My thoughts are rooted in love.

How can you let love guide your thoughts more intentionally today?

_____

_____

_____

_____

_____

_____

_____

_____

_____

_____

_____

Day 80

I am grateful for the power of my mind.

What has your mind helped you create or overcome that deserves celebration?

_____

_____

_____

_____

_____

_____

_____

_____

_____

_____

_____

Day 81

I think with clarity, speak with purpose, and act with integrity.

Where can you bring your thoughts, words, and actions back into alignment?

_____

_____

_____

_____

_____

_____

_____

_____

_____

_____

Day 82

I embrace each new thought as I step forward.

What new empowering thought can you claim today as your next step?

Day 83

I choose empowering stories about myself.

What story about who you are needs to be rewritten?

_____

_____

_____

_____

_____

_____

_____

_____

_____

_____

_____

Day 84

My mindset attracts growth and abundance.

What growth are you most proud of right now?

_____

_____

_____

_____

_____

_____

_____

_____

_____

_____

Day 85

I find solutions with creativity and ease.

What challenge could you solve differently by thinking outside the box?

_____

_____

_____

_____

_____

_____

_____

_____

_____

_____

Day 86

I welcome mental rest and peace.

How can you give your mind permission to rest today?

_____

_____

_____

_____

_____

_____

_____

_____

_____

_____

Day 87

My thoughts align with the woman I am becoming.

What thought today best reflects your next-level self?

_____

_____

_____

_____

_____

_____

_____

_____

_____

_____

Day 88

I free my mind from limitation.

What limiting belief are you ready to let go of for good?

_____

_____

_____

_____

_____

_____

_____

_____

_____

_____

_____

Day 89

I think thoughts that create joy.

What thought instantly makes you smile?

_____

_____

_____

_____

_____

_____

_____

_____

_____

_____

Day 90

My self-belief grows daily.

How can you celebrate the ways you're becoming more confident?

Day 91

I can focus on the positive in every moment.

What's something good that's already present in your life right now?

_____

_____

_____

_____

_____

_____

_____

_____

_____

_____

Day 92

I no longer dwell on the past.

What can you thank the past for and release with peace?

_____

_____

_____

_____

_____

_____

_____

_____

_____

_____

Day 93

My vision for my life is clear.

What step today brings you closer to that vision?

_____

_____

_____

_____

_____

_____

_____

_____

_____

Day 94

I choose to believe in myself.

What proof shows you that you can trust yourself completely?

_____

_____

_____

_____

_____

_____

_____

_____

_____

_____

_____

Day 95

My thoughts align with my Higher Self.

How would your Higher Self handle what you're facing right now?

_____

_____

_____

_____

_____

_____

_____

_____

_____

_____

Day 96

I see challenges as stepping stones.

What growth opportunity is hidden inside your current challenge?

_____

_____

_____

_____

_____

_____

_____

_____

_____

_____

Day 97

I'm a magnet for success.

What success-driven thought can you anchor into today?

Day 98

I am a visionary, and I trust my ideas.

What idea has been waiting for you to take action on it?

_____

_____

_____

_____

_____

_____

_____

_____

_____

_____

_____

Day 99

My mental energy is balanced and strong.

What restores you when you start to feel drained?

_____

_____

_____

_____

_____

_____

_____

_____

_____

_____

Day 100

I let my thoughts serve me, not sabotage me.

What unhelpful thought can you release and replace today?

Day 101

My self-worth is not up for debate.

What would change if you stopped negotiating your value?

_____

_____

_____

_____

_____

_____

_____

_____

_____

_____

Day 102

I think thoughts of hope, love, and possibility.

What possibility excites you the most about your future?

_____

_____

_____

_____

_____

_____

_____

_____

_____

_____

Day 103

I choose to speak kindly to myself.

What kind thing can you say to yourself in this very moment?

Day 104

My mind is open, curious, and clear.

What new experience can you say yes to this week?

_____

_____

_____

_____

_____

_____

_____

_____

_____

_____

Day 105

I believe in new beginnings.

What fresh start are you ready to give yourself permission to take?

_____

_____

_____

_____

_____

_____

_____

_____

_____

_____

Day 106

I release limiting beliefs with grace.

What belief no longer fits who you're becoming?

_____

_____

_____

_____

_____

_____

_____

_____

_____

_____

Day 107

I am free to change my mind and my path.

What would it look like to pivot without guilt or pressure?

_____

_____

_____

_____

_____

_____

_____

_____

_____

_____

_____

Day 108

My thoughts invite abundance.

What abundant thought can you hold as your focus today?

_____

_____

_____

_____

_____

_____

_____

_____

_____

_____

Day 109

I am safe to trust my inner wisdom.

What's your inner voice quietly guiding you to do next?

_____

_____

_____

_____

_____

_____

_____

_____

_____

_____

_____

_____

Day 110

I create success with my thinking, which leads to action.

What successful outcome can you visualize and affirm today?

Day 111

I am free from mental clutter.

What can you simplify to bring peace to your mind?

_____

_____

_____

_____

_____

_____

_____

_____

_____

_____

Day 112

My clarity creates momentum.

What clear next step will move you closer to your goal?

_____

_____

_____

_____

_____

_____

_____

_____

_____

_____

Day 113

I focus on what lights me up.

What brings you genuine joy, and how can you do more of it?

_____

_____

_____

_____

_____

_____

_____

_____

_____

_____

Day 114

I am capable of brilliant ideas.

What idea deserves your attention and confidence right now?

_____

_____

_____

_____

_____

_____

_____

_____

_____

_____

_____

Day 115

My thinking shapes a life I love.

What thought today moves you closer to the life you deserve?

_____

_____

_____

_____

_____

_____

_____

_____

_____

_____

Day 116

I no longer allow fear to dominate my thoughts.

How can you better control your thoughts?

_____

_____

_____

_____

_____

_____

_____

_____

_____

_____

_____

Day 117

I choose to believe in miracles.

What miracle could unfold if you simply stayed open to it?

_____

_____

_____

_____

_____

_____

_____

_____

_____

_____

Day 118

I focus on what I can create today.

What can you build or begin right now with what you already have?

_____

_____

_____

_____

_____

_____

_____

_____

_____

_____

Day 119

I choose happiness daily.

What's one positive outcome you can choose to believe in today?

Day 120

My thoughts are my superpower.

How can you use your thoughts to empower, not limit, yourself today?

Day 121

I am free to let go of overthinking.

What can you decide and move forward on, no more second-guessing?

_____

_____

_____

_____

_____

_____

_____

_____

_____

_____

Day 122

I believe in my unstoppable mind.

What would your next bold step be if you fully trusted your unstoppable mind?

_____

_____

_____

_____

_____

_____

_____

_____

_____

_____

Day 123

My body is my sacred home, and I honor it daily.

What simple ritual will you practice today to honor yourself?

_____

_____

_____

_____

_____

_____

_____

_____

_____

Day 124

I treat my body with love, care, and respect.

How will you show your body respect in the next hour?

_____

_____

_____

_____

_____

_____

_____

_____

_____

_____

Day 125

Every cell in my body vibrates with health and energy.

What energizing choice can you make right now to support your body?

_____

_____

_____

_____

_____

_____

_____

_____

_____

_____

Day 126

I am grateful for the strength my body gives me.

How will you use your physical strength today?

_____

_____

_____

_____

_____

_____

_____

_____

_____

Day 127

I nourish my body with rest, movement, and joy.

Which area needs attention today, and how will you give it?

_____

_____

_____

_____

_____

_____

_____

_____

_____

_____

Day 128

I release judgment of my body and embrace acceptance.

What judgmental thought will you realease?

_____

_____

_____

_____

_____

_____

_____

_____

_____

_____

Day 129

My body is worthy of love at every size and stage.

How will you speak love over your body in the mirror today?

_____

_____

_____

_____

_____

_____

_____

_____

_____

_____

Day 130

I listen to my body and honor its wisdom.

How will you respond to the message your body is sending you?

_____

_____

_____

_____

_____

_____

_____

_____

_____

_____

_____

Day 131

I radiate beauty from the inside out.

What inner quality will you amplify today so it shines through your body?

_____

_____

_____

_____

_____

_____

_____

_____

_____

_____

Day 132

My body is capable of healing and renewal.

What will you do today to support your body's natural healing?

_____

_____

_____

_____

_____

_____

_____

_____

_____

_____

Day 133

I move my body with grace and strength.

What movement will you choose today that feels powerful and graceful?

_____

_____

_____

_____

_____

_____

_____

_____

_____

_____

Day 134

I am grateful for the breath that sustains me.

Pause for three slow, intentional breaths: how did that feel?

_____

_____

_____

_____

_____

_____

_____

_____

_____

_____

_____

Day 135

I celebrate the ways my body supports my life.

What everyday action will you celebrate your body for doing well?

_____

_____

_____

_____

_____

_____

_____

_____

_____

_____

_____

Day 136

My body is enough just as it is.

What activity will you do today without trying to change or fix your body?

Day 137

I treat my body as my partner in life.

How will you collaborate with your body instead of pushing against it today?

_____

_____

_____

_____

_____

_____

_____

_____

_____

_____

Day 138

I trust my body's signals.

Which signal have you been ignoring that you'll honor today?

_____

_____

_____

_____

_____

_____

_____

_____

_____

_____

Day 139

My body deserves kindness and compassion.

What kind gesture will you offer your body before bed tonight?

_____

_____

_____

_____

_____

_____

_____

_____

_____

_____

Day 140

I feel strong and energized in my body.

What 10-minute action will boost your strength or energy right now?

_____

_____

_____

_____

_____

_____

_____

_____

_____

_____

Day 141

My body is a vessel of joy.

What playful movement will you do today just for joy?

_____

_____

_____

_____

_____

_____

_____

_____

_____

_____

Day 142

I respect the journey of my body.

How will you acknowledge a chapter of your body's story with gratitude?

_____

_____

_____

_____

_____

_____

_____

_____

_____

_____

Day 143

My body knows how to heal.

What will you remove from your day to give your body space to heal?

_____

_____

_____

_____

_____

_____

_____

_____

_____

_____

_____

Day 144

I love the skin I am in.

What skin-care or self-touch ritual will you enjoy slowly today?

_____

_____

_____

_____

_____

_____

_____

_____

_____

_____

Day 145

My body supports my dreams.

What body-supporting habit will you stack onto a daily routine?

_____

_____

_____

_____

_____

_____

_____

_____

_____

Day 146

I move my body to feel alive.

What song will you move to today to wake up your aliveness?

_____

_____

_____

_____

_____

_____

_____

_____

_____

_____

Day 147

My body deserves rest when it asks for it.

Where will you schedule a non-negotiable rest window today?

_____

_____

_____

_____

_____

_____

_____

_____

_____

_____

Day 148

I am grateful for my body's resilience.

What evidence of resilience will you name and celebrate right now?

Day 149

My body is a miracle.

Spend five minutes looking in the mirror, naked, and how do you feel looking at yourself?

_____

_____

_____

_____

_____

_____

_____

_____

_____

_____

Day 150

I release shame and embrace my body fully.

What will you wear today that lets you feel free?

_____

_____

_____

_____

_____

_____

_____

_____

_____

_____

Day 151

My body is powerful and sacred.

How will you protect your body's power with a clear boundary today?

Day 152

I am in harmony with my body's rhythms.

What rhythm (sleep, cycle, hunger) will you honor with a gentle adjustment?

_____

_____

_____

_____

_____

_____

_____

_____

_____

_____

_____

Day 153

My body responds to love.

What loving phrase will you repeat to your body three times today?

_____

_____

_____

_____

_____

_____

_____

_____

_____

Day 154

I am grateful for all of my senses.

Which sense, that you have been taking for granted, will you delight in on purpose today, and how?

Day 155

My body glows with vitality.

What will you add to your water or plate to support your glow?

_____

_____

_____

_____

_____

_____

_____

_____

_____

Day 156

I nourish my body with foods that energize me.

What energizing foods are you excited to try?

_____

_____

_____

_____

_____

_____

_____

_____

_____

Day 157

My body is strong and capable.

What strength move (push, pull, squat, carry) will you practice today?

_____

_____

_____

_____

_____

_____

_____

_____

_____

Day 158

I honor my body's cycles.

How will you adjust your pace to match your current cycle or season?

_____

_____

_____

_____

_____

_____

_____

_____

_____

_____

Day 159

My body thrives with movement.

What movement will you schedule between tasks today?

_____

_____

_____

_____

_____

_____

_____

_____

_____

_____

Day 160

I accept my body fully.

What thought will you choose when negative body talk tries to intrude?

Day 161

My body is radiant with health.

How will you support your body today?

Day 162

I am kind to my body.

How will you swap criticism for kindness in your self-talk today?

_____

_____

_____

_____

_____

_____

_____

_____

_____

_____

_____

Day 163

My body is resilient and wise.

What body cue will you follow within the next hour?

_____

_____

_____

_____

_____

_____

_____

_____

_____

_____

Day 164

I trust my body's needs.

What needs, hydration, protein, stretch, sunlight, will you meet now?

_____

_____

_____

_____

_____

_____

_____

_____

_____

_____

Day 165

I am grateful for my body's strength.

Which daily task will you approach as a strength practice?

_____

_____

_____

_____

_____

_____

_____

_____

_____

Day 166

My body is a reflection of my inner love.

What inner loving thought will you anchor before you get dressed?

_____

_____

_____

_____

_____

_____

_____

_____

_____

Day 167

I love and appreciate my body today.

What appreciation note will you write to a specific body part?

_____

_____

_____

_____

_____

_____

_____

_____

_____

_____

Day 168

I am grateful for my body's flexibility.

What gentle stretch will you hold for 60 seconds today?

_____

_____

_____

_____

_____

_____

_____

_____

_____

Day 169

My body is whole and complete.

What will you stop postponing until your body is "different"?

Day 170

I honor the temple of my body.

What boundary will you set around what enters your body today?

_____

_____

_____

_____

_____

_____

_____

_____

_____

_____

Day 171

My body brings me joy.

What joyful sensation will you intentionally savor for 30 seconds?

Day 172

I trust my body's timing.

How will you release urgency and let your body set the pace?

_____

_____

_____

_____

_____

_____

_____

_____

_____

_____

Day 173

My body deserves love daily.

What daily micro-ritual of love will you begin today?

_____

_____

_____

_____

_____

_____

_____

_____

_____

Day 174

I thank my body for carrying me.

Where can you walk today while consciously thanking your body?

_____

_____

_____

_____

_____

_____

_____

_____

_____

_____

Day 175

My body is sacred and powerful.

What powerful posture will you hold for one minute to embody sacred strength?

Day 176

I love every inch of my body.

Which "ignored" area will you pamper with self-love today?

_____

_____

_____

_____

_____

_____

_____

_____

_____

Day 177

My body is safe and supported.

What environment tweak will help your body feel safer?

_____

_____

_____

_____

_____

_____

_____

_____

_____

_____

Day 178

I feel comfortable in my body.

What will you wear or adjust to increase physical comfort right now?

_____

_____

_____

_____

_____

_____

_____

_____

_____

_____

Day 179

My body is alive with energy.

What quick energizer, cold splash, brisk walk, stairs, will you do?

_____

_____

_____

_____

_____

_____

_____

_____

_____

_____

Day 180

I am grateful for my body's wisdom.

What pattern has your body shown you that you'll honor today?

_____

_____

_____

_____

_____

_____

_____

_____

_____

_____

Day 181

My body empowers me daily.

What action will you take today because your body enables it?

Day 182

I honor my body's voice.

When will you pause to ask, "Body, what do you need?" and listen?

_____

_____

_____

_____

_____

_____

_____

_____

_____

_____

_____

Day 183

My body is worthy of rest.

What bedtime cue will you protect tonight to improve your sleep?

_____

_____

_____

_____

_____

_____

_____

_____

_____

_____

Day 184

I am grateful for my body's endurance.

What steady, sustainable movement will you practice today?

_____

_____

_____

_____

_____

_____

_____

_____

_____

_____

Day 185

My body deserves care and love.

Which appointment or routine care will you schedule this week?

_____

_____

_____

_____

_____

_____

_____

_____

_____

_____

Day 186

My body is beautiful in every way.

What compliment will you give yourself out loud today?

_____

_____

_____

_____

_____

_____

_____

_____

_____

_____

Day 187

I move my body with joy.

What fun, low-pressure movement will you do for five minutes?

_____

_____

_____

_____

_____

_____

_____

_____

_____

_____

Day 188

My body brings me freedom.

Where will you choose to move today simply because you can?

_____

_____

_____

_____

_____

_____

_____

_____

_____

_____

Day 189

I listen to my body with compassion.

How will you respond gently when your body says "not today"?

_____

_____

_____

_____

_____

_____

_____

_____

_____

Day 190

My body is at peace.

What relaxation practice will you do for three minutes right now?

_____

_____

_____

_____

_____

_____

_____

_____

_____

_____

Day 191

My body is vibrant and alive.

What color-rich food or outdoor moment will you choose to feel more alive?

_____

_____

_____

_____

_____

_____

_____

_____

_____

_____

_____

Day 192

I celebrate my body's uniqueness.

What unique feature will you highlight and celebrate today?

_____

_____

_____

_____

_____

_____

_____

_____

_____

_____

Day 193

My body is a gift.

How will you treat your body like a treasured gift today?

_____

_____

_____

_____

_____

_____

_____

_____

_____

_____

_____

Day 194

I am grateful for my healthy body.

What health-supporting choice will you prioritize before noon?

_____

_____

_____

_____

_____

_____

_____

_____

_____

_____

Day 195

My body radiates confidence.

What confident stance or stride will you embody in your next interaction?

_____

_____

_____

_____

_____

_____

_____

_____

_____

_____

_____

Day 196

I trust my body's signals of rest and movement.

When will you schedule alternating blocks for focused work and movement?

_____

_____

_____

_____

_____

_____

_____

_____

_____

_____

Day 197

My body thrives when I care for it.

What is one healing modality you've been curious to try? Go do it!

_____

_____

_____

_____

_____

_____

_____

_____

_____

_____

Day 198

My body is aligned with wellness.

What one alignment, posture, hydration, meal timing, will you refine today?

_____

_____

_____

_____

_____

_____

_____

_____

_____

_____

Day 199

I honor the miracle of my body.

What will you pause to observe that reminds you your body is perfect as it is?

_____

_____

_____

_____

_____

_____

_____

_____

_____

Day 200

My body is my ally.

What will you stop saying or doing that turns your ally into an enemy?

_____

_____

_____

_____

_____

_____

_____

_____

_____

_____

_____

_____

Day 201

My body responds with vitality.

What vitality-boosting choice will you repeat tomorrow?

_____

_____

_____

_____

_____

_____

_____

_____

_____

_____

Day 202

I thank my body for carrying my soul.

How will you move today in a way that feels soulful?

_____

_____

_____

_____

_____

_____

_____

_____

_____

_____

Day 203

My body radiates love.

What loving action will you take toward your body before leaving the house?

_____

_____

_____

_____

_____

_____

_____

_____

_____

_____

Day 204

I embrace the journey my body has taken.

What past chapter of your body's journey will you bless and release?

_____

_____

_____

_____

_____

_____

_____

_____

_____

_____

Day 205

My body is resilient through change.

What supportive routine will you keep steady while things shift?

_____

_____

_____

_____

_____

_____

_____

_____

_____

_____

Day 206

My body deserves joy.

What delightfully "extra" body treat will you gift yourself today?

_____

_____

_____

_____

_____

_____

_____

_____

_____

_____

_____

Day 207

I feel grounded in my body.

What grounding practice, barefoot earth, wall sit, slow breath, will you do?

_____

_____

_____

_____

_____

_____

_____

_____

_____

_____

Day 208

My body is my sanctuary.

What will you remove from your space to keep your area calm?

_____

_____

_____

_____

_____

_____

_____

_____

_____

_____

Day 209

I listen with love to my body's whispers.

What whisper will you act on before it has to become a shout?

_____

_____

_____

_____

_____

_____

_____

_____

_____

_____

Day 210

My body is whole and sacred.

What sacred pause will you weave into a busy moment today?

_____

_____

_____

_____

_____

_____

_____

_____

_____

_____

Day 211

I am grateful for my body's adaptability.

Where will you flex your routine to meet your body's current needs?

_____

_____

_____

_____

_____

_____

_____

_____

_____

_____

Day 212

My body supports my dreams with strength.

What dream-aligned physical habit will you practice today?

_____

_____

_____

_____

_____

_____

_____

_____

_____

_____

Day 213

I move my body to celebrate life.

How will you celebrate something small with a movement break?

_____

_____

_____

_____

_____

_____

_____

_____

_____

_____

_____

Day 214

My body is divine creation.

What will you do to experience awe in your own design today?

_____

_____

_____

_____

_____

_____

_____

_____

_____

_____

Day 215

I feel safe in my body.

What boundary or comfort cue will you set to reinforce safety?

_____

_____

_____

_____

_____

_____

_____

_____

_____

_____

Day 216

My body is worthy of my love.

What concrete act of love will you give your body this afternoon?

_____

_____

_____

_____

_____

_____

_____

_____

_____

_____

Day 217

My body flourishes with care.

What care routine will you simplify so it actually happens?

_____

_____

_____

_____

_____

_____

_____

_____

_____

_____

Day 218

I celebrate the gift of movement.

Which movement will you choose that your future self will thank you for?

_____

_____

_____

_____

_____

_____

_____

_____

_____

_____

Day 219

My body glows with self-love.

What self-love ritual will you do tonight to support your glow?

_____

_____

_____

_____

_____

_____

_____

_____

_____

_____

Day 220

I am grateful for my body's voice.

How will you capture and honor one message your body gives today?

_____

_____

_____

_____

_____

_____

_____

_____

_____

_____

Day 221

My body radiates balance.

What will in your life will you rebalance, today?

Day 222

I love how my body feels.

What slight shift will make your body feel 10% better right now?

_____

_____

_____

_____

_____

_____

_____

_____

_____

_____

_____

Day 223

My body is strong, flexible, and capable.

Which of the three: strength, flexibility, or capability, will you train today?

_____

_____

_____

_____

_____

_____

_____

_____

_____

_____

Day 224

My body carries me with grace.

How will you move more gently between tasks today?

_____

_____

_____

_____

_____

_____

_____

_____

_____

_____

Day 225

I release judgment and honor my body.

What negative self-talk needs to be replaced to honor myself?

_____

_____

_____

_____

_____

_____

_____

_____

_____

_____

Day 226

My body is a friend, not an enemy.

What friendly gesture will you extend to your body when it's tired?

_____

_____

_____

_____

_____

_____

_____

_____

_____

_____

Day 227

My body deserves compassion.

When will you choose gentleness over pushing through?

_____

_____

_____

_____

_____

_____

_____

_____

_____

_____

Day 228

I am grateful for my body's energy.

What will you do to protect your energy from leaks today?

_____

_____

_____

_____

_____

_____

_____

_____

_____

_____

Day 229

My body thrives with gratitude.

What gratitude practice will you pair with meals or movement?

_____

_____

_____

_____

_____

_____

_____

_____

_____

_____

Day 230

My body is sacred ground.

What will you stop allowing into this space that doesn't honor who you're becoming?

_____

_____

_____

_____

_____

_____

_____

_____

_____

_____

Day 231

My body brings me home to myself.

What grounding cue will you use to return to your body during stress?

_____

_____

_____

_____

_____

_____

_____

_____

_____

_____

Day 232

I love how my body moves.

Which movement feels delicious today, and when will you do it?

_____

_____

_____

_____

_____

_____

_____

_____

_____

Day 233

My body is radiant with joy.

What joyful activity will you schedule like an appointment?

_____

_____

_____

_____

_____

_____

_____

_____

_____

Day 234

I treat my body with gentleness.

When will you slow your pace to practice gentle care?

_____

_____

_____

_____

_____

_____

_____

_____

_____

_____

Day 235

My body gives me freedom.

What freedom will you claim with your body today, walk, dance, play?

_____

_____

_____

_____

_____

_____

_____

_____

_____

_____

Day 236

I celebrate my body's power.

What personal record or mini-challenge will you attempt today?

_____

_____

_____

_____

_____

_____

_____

_____

_____

_____

Day 237

My body heals in perfect timing.

What will you stop rushing so your body can repair at its own pace?

_____

_____

_____

_____

_____

_____

_____

_____

_____

_____

Day 238

I embrace my body fully.

What part of your body will you admire out loud today?

_____

_____

_____

_____

_____

_____

_____

_____

_____

_____

_____

Day 239

My body is an expression of my spirit.

What soulful practice will you embody through movement or posture?

_____

_____

_____

_____

_____

_____

_____

_____

_____

_____

_____

_____

Day 240

I am grateful for the gift of embodiment.

What sensory experience will you savor slowly, taste, touch, sound, sight, smell?

_____

_____

_____

_____

_____

_____

_____

_____

_____

_____

Day 241

My body deserves daily care.

What daily care task will you add to an existing habit?

_____

_____

_____

_____

_____

_____

_____

_____

_____

_____

Day 242

My body radiates health.

What one upgrade will you make today?

_____

_____

_____

_____

_____

_____

_____

_____

_____

_____

Day 243

I trust and love my body deeply.

What promise will you make to your body and keep today?

_____

_____

_____

_____

_____

_____

_____

_____

_____

_____

Day 244

My body is my sacred home.

What closing ritual will you do tonight to thank your body for carrying you?

_____

_____

_____

_____

_____

_____

_____

_____

_____

_____

Day 245

My soul is rooted in love and guided by light.

What can you do today that reflects love and light in action?

_____

_____

_____

_____

_____

_____

_____

_____

_____

_____

_____

Day 246

I trust the divine timing of my life.

Where will you release control and trust that God/Source/Universe already has it handled?

_____

_____

_____

_____

_____

_____

_____

_____

_____

_____

_____

_____

Day 247

I am deeply connected to my higher self.

What quiet practice helps you hear the voice of your higher self clearly?

_____

_____

_____

_____

_____

_____

_____

_____

_____

_____

_____

Day 248

My soul knows peace, even when my mind races.

When your thoughts feel loud, how will you ground yourself back into peace?

_____

_____

_____

_____

_____

_____

_____

_____

_____

_____

_____

Day 249

I am aligned with the purpose of my existence.

What choice can you make today that aligns with why you're truly here?

_____

_____

_____

_____

_____

_____

_____

_____

_____

_____

Day 250

Love flows through me and touches everyone around me.

What act of kindness can you show to someone in need today?

_____

_____

_____

_____

_____

_____

_____

_____

_____

_____

Day 251

I am divinely protected and supported.

Where can you stop striving and let divine support carry you?

_____

_____

_____

_____

_____

_____

_____

_____

_____

_____

Day 252

I embrace the whispers of my soul and follow them boldly.

What inner nudge have you been ignoring that deserves brave action today?

_____

_____

_____

_____

_____

_____

_____

_____

_____

_____

_____

_____

Day 253

My spirit is unbreakable, no matter what may come.

What truth will you lean into when life feels heavy?

_____

_____

_____

_____

_____

_____

_____

_____

_____

_____

_____

Day 254

I am connected to something greater than myself.

How can you reconnect to your Higher Power right now?

_____

_____

_____

_____

_____

_____

_____

_____

_____

_____

_____

Day 255

My soul radiates kindness, compassion, and strength.

Where can you extend kindness that costs you nothing but changes everything?

_____

_____

_____

_____

_____

_____

_____

_____

_____

Day 256

I am a vessel of love, healing, and light.

What healing energy can you share with someone who needs it today?

Day 257

My soul shines with authenticity.

What mask are you ready to take off to let your true self shine?

_____

_____

_____

_____

_____

_____

_____

_____

_____

_____

Day 258

I trust the journey of my soul.

Where can you replace anxiety with faith that your soul already knows the way?

_____

_____

_____

_____

_____

_____

_____

_____

_____

_____

_____

_____

Day 259

I am aligned with divine wisdom.

What decision will you pause on until you feel divine clarity?

Day 260

My spirit radiates joy.

What small thing will you do today just for the joy of it?

_____

_____

_____

_____

_____

_____

_____

_____

_____

_____

Day 261

I am deeply loved by the Universe.

How can you receive love today without guilt or resistance?

_____

_____

_____

_____

_____

_____

_____

_____

_____

_____

_____

Day 262

My soul is free to express itself fully.

What creative or spiritual expression have you been holding back?

_____

_____

_____

_____

_____

_____

_____

_____

_____

_____

_____

Day 263

I listen to my soul's wisdom.

What truth is your soul asking you to honor today?

_____

_____

_____

_____

_____

_____

_____

_____

_____

_____

Day 264

I am in harmony with my soul's purpose.

What activity today will bring you into deeper harmony with your calling?

_____

_____

_____

_____

_____

_____

_____

_____

_____

_____

_____

Day 265

My soul expands with gratitude.

What blessing will you stop and fully
appreciate right now?

_____

_____

_____

_____

_____

_____

_____

_____

_____

_____

Day 266

I trust the unfolding of my soul's path.

What expectation can you release to make room for what's unfolding?

_____

_____

_____

_____

_____

_____

_____

_____

_____

_____

_____

Day 267

My soul radiates peace.

What peaceful habit will you protect in your daily routine?

_____

_____

_____

_____

_____

_____

_____

_____

_____

_____

Day 268

I am whole in my soul.

What story of "not enough" are you ready to release today?

_____

_____

_____

_____

_____

_____

_____

_____

_____

_____

_____

Day 269

My spirit shines brighter each day.

What thought, word, or action will help your spirit shine today?

_____

_____

_____

_____

_____

_____

_____

_____

_____

_____

Day 270

I trust the divine guidance of my soul.

How will you act on the guidance that keeps repeating itself in your heart?

Day 271

My soul is timeless and wise.

What past experience still holds wisdom for your present moment?

_____

_____

_____

_____

_____

_____

_____

_____

_____

_____

Day 272

I am connected to infinite love.

How will you let infinite love flow through you today?

_____

_____

_____

_____

_____

_____

_____

_____

_____

_____

Day 273

My soul guides me home.

What does "home" feel like to you, and how will you return to it today?

_____

_____

_____

_____

_____

_____

_____

_____

_____

_____

Day 274

I embrace the evolution of my soul.

What old version of you are you ready to lovingly let go?

_____

_____

_____

_____

_____

_____

_____

_____

_____

_____

Day 275

My spirit is eternal and limitless.

How will you stop thinking small and honor your limitless nature?

_____

_____

_____

_____

_____

_____

_____

_____

_____

_____

Day 276

I radiate divine love.

What loving action can you take that reminds someone they matter?

_____

_____

_____

_____

_____

_____

_____

_____

_____

_____

_____

Day 277

My soul is a source of endless strength.

What challenge will you face today, knowing your strength is enough?

_____

_____

_____

_____

_____

_____

_____

_____

_____

_____

_____

Day 278

I honor my soul's journey, and let go of control.

How will you celebrate how far your soul has already come?

_____

_____

_____

_____

_____

_____

_____

_____

_____

_____

_____

Day 279

I am aligned with higher love.

What relationship or habit will you raise to the frequency of love?

_____

_____

_____

_____

_____

_____

_____

_____

_____

_____

Day 280

My spirit thrives in freedom.

What boundary will you set to protect your spiritual freedom?

_____

_____

_____

_____

_____

_____

_____

_____

_____

_____

_____

Day 281

My soul radiates divine truth.

What truth will you stop hiding and finally own?

_____

_____

_____

_____

_____

_____

_____

_____

_____

_____

_____

Day 282

I trust the light within me.

When doubt appears, how will you remind yourself that your light never dims?

_____

_____

_____

_____

_____

_____

_____

_____

_____

_____

Day 283

My soul whispers wisdom daily.

What can you do this morning to slow down
and actually hear that whisper?

_____

_____

_____

_____

_____

_____

_____

_____

_____

_____

_____

Day 284

I am guided by divine love.

What decision today will you make from love, not fear?

_____

_____

_____

_____

_____

_____

_____

_____

_____

_____

Day 285

My spirit is free and expansive.

What can you do to release the weight of
anything that feels restrictive?

_____

_____

_____

_____

_____

_____

_____

_____

_____

_____

Day 286

My soul is a mirror of divine love.

How can you reflect divine love back into the world today?

_____

_____

_____

_____

_____

_____

_____

_____

_____

_____

Day 287

I honor the sacred within me.

What sacred moment will you create for yourself before the day ends?

_____

_____

_____

_____

_____

_____

_____

_____

_____

_____

Day 288

My soul flourishes with authenticity.

Where can you show up more real and less rehearsed?

_____

_____

_____

_____

_____

_____

_____

_____

_____

_____

_____

_____

Day 289

I honor my ancestor's for guiding me in my journey.

How can you stop and pay your ancestors respect right now?

_____

_____

_____

_____

_____

_____

_____

_____

_____

_____

Day 290

My spirit connects me with all life.

What act of kindness can you offer to someone or something in your environment?

_____

_____

_____

_____

_____

_____

_____

_____

_____

_____

Day 291

I shine from my soul outward.

What intention will you set so your inner light leads the way?

_____

_____

_____

_____

_____

_____

_____

_____

_____

_____

Day 292

I trust my inner light.

When was the last time you followed your intuition, and will you do it again today?

Day 293

My soul expands through love.

How can you expand your love to include someone you've been holding back from?

_____

_____

_____

_____

_____

_____

_____

_____

_____

_____

Day 294

I am deeply connected to Spirit.

What spiritual practice will you prioritize to strengthen that connection?

_____

_____

_____

_____

_____

_____

_____

_____

_____

_____

_____

_____

Day 295

My soul sings with freedom.

What will you release today that lets your soul breathe easier?

_____

_____

_____

_____

_____

_____

_____

_____

_____

_____

_____

Day 296

I am a divine expression of love.

How can you embody love in your next conversation or action?

_____

_____

_____

_____

_____

_____

_____

_____

_____

_____

Day 297

My spirit is pure and radiant.

What habit or thought will you cleanse from your energy today?

Day 298

I trust my sacred path.

Where and how will you take one step forward, even when you can't see the full road?

_____

_____

_____

_____

_____

_____

_____

_____

_____

_____

_____

Day 299

My soul reflects infinite wisdom.

What life lesson will you finally apply instead of just remembering?

_____

_____

_____

_____

_____

_____

_____

_____

_____

_____

_____

Day 300

I embrace the divine light in me.

What moment today can you use to shine without shrinking?

_____

_____

_____

_____

_____

_____

_____

_____

_____

_____

Day 301

My spirit is boundless and free.

What boundary or belief are you ready to expand on?

_____

_____

_____

_____

_____

_____

_____

_____

_____

_____

Day 302

I trust in divine alignment.

What aligned action can you take that feels guided, not forced?

_____

_____

_____

_____

_____

_____

_____

_____

_____

_____

Day 303

My soul is love in action.

How will you turn love into a tangible act today?

_____

_____

_____

_____

_____

_____

_____

_____

_____

_____

_____

Day 304

I am guided by spirit daily.

How will you make space to listen before moving today?

_____

_____

_____

_____

_____

_____

_____

_____

_____

_____

Day 305

My soul flourishes in truth.

What truth have you been avoiding that your soul wants you to face?

_____

_____

_____

_____

_____

_____

_____

_____

_____

Day 306

I embrace the Goddess within me.

How can you show up today like a woman who knows she is a Goddess?

_____

_____

_____

_____

_____

_____

_____

_____

_____

_____

_____

Day 307

My spirit radiates eternal light.

Where will you shine that eternal light to uplift others today?

_____

_____

_____

_____

_____

_____

_____

_____

_____

_____

_____

Day 308

I trust the infinite wisdom of my soul.

What soul-led decision have you been delaying that needs action now?

_____

_____

_____

_____

_____

_____

_____

_____

_____

_____

_____

Day 309

My soul is my true compass.

What direction does your soul keep pointing you toward, and will you follow it?

_____

_____

_____

_____

_____

_____

_____

_____

_____

_____

_____

Day 310

I embody divine love.

What does embodying love look like in your choices and boundaries today?

_____

_____

_____

_____

_____

_____

_____

_____

_____

Day 311

My spirit is unshakable.

What grounded practice will keep you steady when life tries to shake you?

_____

_____

_____

_____

_____

_____

_____

_____

_____

_____

Day 312

I am safe in divine presence.

Where can you release fear knowing you are never alone?

_____

_____

_____

_____

_____

_____

_____

_____

_____

_____

_____

Day 313

My soul glows with peace.

What will you do today to protect that peaceful glow?

_____

_____

_____

_____

_____

_____

_____

_____

_____

_____

Day 314

I am a channel of love.

What does love mean to you?

_____

_____

_____

_____

_____

_____

_____

_____

_____

_____

Day 315

My spirit thrives with generosity.

How will you live more truthfully in your relationships today?

_____

_____

_____

_____

_____

_____

_____

_____

_____

_____

Day 316

I am grounded in who I am becoming.

What ritual helps you reconnect with the divine essence within you?

_____

_____

_____

_____

_____

_____

_____

_____

_____
_____

_____

Day 317

My peace cannot be disturbed by chaos.

What will you welcome into your inner sanctuary, and what must go?

_____

_____

_____

_____

_____

_____

_____

_____

_____

_____

_____

Day 318

I trust what life is teaching me.

How can you see yourself today the way the Divine sees you?

_____

_____

_____

_____

_____

_____

_____

_____

_____

_____

_____

Day 319

Every breath reminds me I am enough.

What would you do differently if you truly believed nothing could limit you?

_____

_____

_____

_____

_____

_____

_____

_____

_____

Day 320

I trust the clarity and calmness within.

Where will you slow down or speed up to match your soul's rhythm?

_____

_____

_____

_____

_____

_____

_____

_____

_____

_____

Day 321

My soul is free from fear.

What fear are you ready to release once and for all?

_____

_____

_____

_____

_____

_____

_____

_____

_____

_____

Day 322

I rise each day with quiet and powerful strength.

How can you embody love in how you treat yourself today?

_____

_____

_____

_____

_____

_____

_____

_____

_____

_____

_____

Day 323

My spirit is full of light and it leads me toward truth.

What can you do to share that light with someone 20 years younger and 20 years older?

_____

_____

_____

_____

_____

_____

_____

_____

_____

_____

Day 324

I am guided by the whispers of spirit.

What whisper are you being called to act on before doubt steps in?

_____

_____

_____

_____

_____

_____

_____

_____

_____

_____

_____

Day 325

My inner wisdom knows the next right step.

What morning habit helps your soul radiate its divine energy all day?

_____

_____

_____

_____

_____

_____

_____

_____

_____

_____

Day 326

Nothing outside of me defines my worth.

What will you stand firm in today that reflects your power?

_____

_____

_____

_____

_____

_____

_____

_____

_____

_____

Day 327

My spirit is forever expansive.

How can you stretch beyond what once felt impossible?

_____

_____

_____

_____

_____

_____

_____

_____

_____

_____

Day 328

Strength and softness can coexist within me.

What daily ritual will help you return to that infinite peace within?

_____

_____

_____

_____

_____

_____

_____

_____

_____

_____

_____

Day 329

I permit myself to expand freely.

How can you raise your vibration through your thoughts and actions today?

_____

_____

_____

_____

_____

_____

_____

_____

_____

_____

_____

Day 330

Healing flows through every part of my life.

Where will you allow grace to meet you instead of striving?

_____

_____

_____

_____

_____

_____

_____

_____

_____

_____

_____

Day 331

I move with intention and confidence.

What truth about yourself are you finally ready to live out loud?

_____

_____

_____

_____

_____

_____

_____

_____

_____

_____

_____

Day 332

My light is steady even in transition.

What small act of faith will you take to open the door for miracles?

_____

_____

_____

_____

_____

_____

_____

_____

_____

_____

Day 333

I am the author of my own renewal.

How can you act on what your heart's been whispering for far too long?

Day 334

My spirit transcends fear.

What brave move will remind fear that it no longer runs the show?

_____

_____

_____

_____

_____

_____

_____

_____

_____

_____

_____

Day 335

I am one with divine energy.

How can you ground into oneness before you start your day?

_____

_____

_____

_____

_____

_____

_____

_____

_____

_____

Day 336

My past prepared me for this version of me.

How will you embody light when challenges arise today?

_____

_____

_____

_____

_____

_____

_____

_____

_____

_____

_____

Day 337

I am not responsible for managing anyone else's emotions.

What safety or peace practice will help you stay rooted in your light?

_____

_____

_____

_____

_____

_____

_____

_____

_____

_____

Day 338

Choosing myself is not self-fish, it's self-respect.

How will you make space to listen and follow your spirit's direction today?

_____

_____

_____

_____

_____

_____

_____

_____

_____

_____

Day 339

The patterns that once bound my lineage end with me.

What ancestral strength or lesson will you carry forward with intention?

_____

_____

_____

_____

_____

_____

_____

_____

_____

_____

_____

Day 340

What feels like delay is often preparation for something greater.

What morning action helps you rise awake in both body and spirit?

_____

_____

_____

_____

_____

_____

_____

_____

_____

_____

_____

Day 341

I am safe within my own mind.

What decision can you make today purely from inner knowing?

_____

_____

_____

_____

_____

_____

_____

_____

_____

_____

Day 342

I breathe through discomfort and find clarity on the other side.

How can you let love be the language you use with yourself today?

_____

_____

_____

_____

_____

_____

_____

_____

_____

_____

_____

Day 343

Each day, I grow stronger in how I handle life's ups and downs.

What courageous action will you take that honors your soul's expansion?

_____

_____

_____

_____

_____

_____

_____

_____

_____

_____

_____

Day 344

I release the need to overthink and welcome ease into my mind.

What grounding ritual reconnects you to that anchor when life feels shaky?

_____

_____

_____

_____

_____

_____

_____

_____

_____

_____

Day 345

My spirit is powerful and eternal.

How can you use your eternal power to create something meaningful today?

Day 346

I honor my soul's truth.

What truth will you choose to honor even if it costs you comfort?

_____

_____

_____

_____

_____

_____

_____

_____

_____

_____

_____

Day 347

My soul carries infinite wisdom.

What moment from your past holds a message your present self needs?

_____

_____

_____

_____

_____

_____

_____

_____

_____

_____

_____

Day 348

I shine my soul's light fearlessly.

What fear will you walk through to let your light fully shine?

_____

_____

_____

_____

_____

_____

_____

_____

_____

_____

Day 349

My spirit is filled with gratitude.

Who or what will you thank today with your actions, not just your words?

_____

_____

_____

_____

_____

_____

_____

_____

_____

_____

Day 350

Every season of my life holds purpose and meaning.

What will you do today to live like the divine being you are?

_____

_____

_____

_____

_____

_____

_____

_____

_____

_____

_____

_____

Day 351

My soul breathes love into every moment.

How can you pause and breathe love into the moment you're in right now?

_____

_____

_____

_____

_____

_____

_____

_____

_____

_____

_____

Day 352

My connection to something greater keeps me centered.

Where can you soften and let life unfold naturally today?

_____

_____

_____

_____

_____

_____

_____

_____

_____

_____

Day 353

My spirit radiates compassion.

Who needs your compassion today, even if it's you?

_____

_____

_____

_____

_____

_____

_____

_____

_____

_____

Day 354

I am whole in my soul's light.

What would change if you stopped trying to fix what's already whole?

_____

_____

_____

_____

_____

_____

_____

_____

_____

_____

_____

Day 355

My soul is timeless and radiant.

What timeless truth about you needs to be celebrated right now?

_____

_____

_____

_____

_____

_____

_____

_____

_____

_____

_____

Day 356

I honor the sacred within and around me.

What sacred ritual will you practice today to honor both?

_____

_____

_____

_____

_____

_____

_____

_____

_____

_____

Day 357

I am committed to becoming wiser, calmer, and more aligned each day.

What truth will you speak that frees both you and others?

_____

_____

_____

_____

_____

_____

_____

_____

_____

_____

Day 358

My soul guides me to freedom.

What limitation will you release today to step into your freedom?

_____

_____

_____

_____

_____

_____

_____

_____

_____

_____

Day 359

I am a vessel of divine love.

How can you let love pour through you today?

_____

_____

_____

_____

_____

_____

_____

_____

_____

_____

Day 360

My soul lights the way forward.

What next step feels illuminated by your soul's light?

_____

_____

_____

_____

_____

_____

_____

_____

_____

_____

_____

Day 361

My spirit rises above all fear.

What will you choose today that fear told you not to?

_____

_____

_____

_____

_____

_____

_____

_____

_____

_____

Day 362

I no longer fight every lesson: I learn what life is trying to show me.

What grounding affirmation will you repeat when chaos tries to pull you out of peace?

_____

_____

_____

_____

_____

_____

_____

_____

_____

_____

_____

Day 363

My soul is alive with infinite possibilities.

What possibility excites your soul enough to take the first step now?

_____

_____

_____

_____

_____

_____

_____

_____

_____

_____

_____

Day 364

I radiate divine truth, love, and freedom.

How will you embody truth, love, and freedom in one bold action today?

_____

_____

_____

_____

_____

_____

_____

_____

_____

_____

_____

Day 365

I am whole: mind, body, and soul.

What daily practice will help you keep all parts of you in sacred harmony?

Bonus Leap Year

I boldly walk in my feminine energy, unapologetically!

How will you show up today fully expressed in your feminine power, without shrinking, explaining, or asking permission?

_____

_____

_____

_____

_____

_____

_____

_____

_____

_____

_____

Reflection time

Year-End Reflection

Take a few quiet moments to reflect on the following questions:

Which area spoke to your heart the most this year: *mind, body, or soul?*

_____

_____

_____

_____

_____

_____

_____

_____

_____

_____

In what ways has your mind, body, or soul grown stronger?

_____

_____

_____

_____

_____

_____

_____

_____

What old beliefs or patterns have you finally released?

_____

_____

_____

_____

What does being rooted, empowered, awakened, and liberated mean to you?

What blessing will you carry forward as your guiding light?

Closing yearly blessing...

As you stand at the end of these 365 days of affirmations, take a breath and honor yourself. You chose to show up. For your mind, for your body, and for your soul. Every word you spoke over yourself this year has planted seeds of healing, courage, and liberation.

I bless you with clarity of mind, so your thoughts forever align with truth, peace, and possibility.

I bless you with love and respect for your body, so you move through life rooted in strength, confidence, and joy.

I bless you with the radiance of your soul, so your spirit shines in every room you enter and lights the path for those who walk behind you.

May you rise into the fullness of who you are: a woman who dares, a woman who heals, a woman who leads, a free woman.

May every step forward be guided by grace, every challenge be met with resilience, and every dream unfold in divine timing.
And as you carry this book into another year, may it remind you daily of this unshakable truth:

You are whole. You are worthy. You are liberated.

With love & light,
Maryann

About the author

Dr. Maryann Rivera-Dannert is the CEO of MRD Empowerment Solutions, LLC, which is for the Woman who's ready to HEAL and turn her FEAR into fuel for SUCCESS. She is a speaker, author, podcast host, and certified life coach dedicated to guiding women on their journey from limitation to a life filled with liberation, purpose, and passion.

Her story is one of resilience and triumph, shaped by personal challenges that could have kept her stuck but instead propelled her forward.

As the author of 20+ published anthologies and two journals, her writing serves as a source of inspiration and practical guidance. Each piece reflects her commitment to helping others navigate their own challenges. In early 2025, she published her first solo book: *From Limitation to Liberation: 50 Mindset Shifts for Women Who Dare*. Maryann also launched a podcast, "Fearless Fridays with Maryann," which provides a platform for meaningful conversations about life, motivation, hope, and personal/professional growth. The podcast has been renamed: Healing*Her* Within, demonstrating growth, and more!

Maryann has a bachelor's degree from Roberts Wesleyan University, a master's from Palm Beach Atlantic University, and an Honorary Doctorate from Trinity International University of Ambassadors (T.I.U.A.). Additionally, she is certified by the John C. Maxwell Certification Program as a Coach, Speaker, and Trainer. Lastly, she recently became a Certified Professional Speaker through the Global Speakers University.

Maryann loves the beach, traveling, and spending time with her family in Rochester, NY.

She may be contacted at: maryann@maryannriveradannert.com

www.ingramcontent.com/pod-product-compliance
Lightning Source LLC
Chambersburg PA
CBHW060106170426
43198CB00010B/788